For the Complete Emancipation of Women in Socialist Society
Ramiz Alia

ISBN: 978-1-387-92269-7

2022 Independent Publisher

Charleroi, PA USA

For the Complete Emancipation of Women in Socialist Society

Ramiz Alia

CONTENTS

INTRODUCTION

This speech was delivered at the 2nd Plenum of the Central Committee of the Party of Labor of Albania on June 15, 1967.

The historic decisions of the 5th Party Congress and the speech Comrade Enver Hoxha delivered on February 6, this year in Tirana furthered the revolutionary spirit which has characterized and characterizes our Party and people. Under the leadership of the Party and the inspiring influence of these, its important documents, our country has been gripped by self-denying work and major revolutionary enthusiasm to build socialism. In this atmosphere new initiatives and profound revolutionary movements have sprung up and have been quickly embraced by urban and rural people of all walks of life in the field of developing production and, in particular, in the ideological field, which are transforming the conscience of people, their Weltanschauung and concepts about many problems and manifestations of our social life.

Among revolutionary movements and initiatives taken so far that of achieving the complete emancipation of women is of foremost importance. It has now gripped all the people, men and women, old and young and has spread to all regions of the country. The mass popular movements of the emancipation of women, the numerous initiatives taken against mediaeval survivals and customs that degraded women, that curbed their personality and made their lives unbearable, should be viewed as a new outburst of revolutionary zeal of colossal importance.

The movement for the emancipation of women in our country, as part and parcel of socialist revolution as a whole, has now made major progress and marks a new qualitative leap forward. This leap is manifested not only in the unprecedented proportions and variety of forms it has taken but, more particularly, in the revolutionary ideologic substance of the present movement for the emancipation of women. Its essence lies in the fact that the conservative, patriarchal, feudal and bourgeois concepts are being ultimately broken and revolutionary concepts about women and their role in society are gaining ground and that the old ideology of the exploiting classes in this field are being smashed and socialist ideology is winning.

Now, the struggle for the emancipation of women is being waged and every day more lively not only by activists and most progressive sector of the population and of youth, in particular, but also by such social forces which, in spite of their incontestable political loyalty to the Party and people's rule, towards the problem of women have so far maintained an attitude of indifference, passivity and even of conservatism. This is borne out by the mass participation of men and women, especially, of those advanced in age at the numerous meetings and conventions that have taken place everywhere in the country, at the mountainous regions of Kukes and Shkodra, of Tirana and Mati, of Tropoja and Berati, of Peshkopia and Korça, of Mallakastra and Lezha at which the past was fearlessly criticized and condemned, at which they pledged their word and entered into an engagement to do away with the survivals of customs and canons, of religious beliefs and every bizarre conduct that oppressed women and lowered their dignity, at which they assure that they would see to it that the sacred law of the Party *"protect the rights of women and girls"* is enforced to the letter.

Participating in the present movement

for the emancipation of women are most of the women themselves and, especially the young women including the women and girls of those mountainous and other regions where women have had to bear most of the weight of backward customs, canons and religious prejudices. Women everywhere have risen and, giving vent to resentments accumulated in their hearts through centuries against every alien thing that lowered their dignity and denied them their rights, have embarked on a bitter struggle for their complete emancipation and to render a fuller contribution, side by side with their menfolk to the prosperity and progress of our socialist homeland. Thousands of mountaineer young women and grown-ups are engaged in volunteer work at the mass actions of youth; many others from cities and lowlands like those of Myzeqeja, Shkodra, Korça and Gjinokastra have expressed their wishes to go to mountain regions for the purpose of conveying to their mates the experience and revolutionary drive which characterizes them in their productive work, in their struggle for the emancipation of women and so on.

The main objective of the movement for the complete emancipation of women is to fight against the survivals of bourgeois, feudal and patriarchal ideology, to fight against old, outworn reactionary concepts on women which constitute one of the main obstacles to their complete emancipation and their real parity with their partners. Of particular significance is the fact that this struggle and consequently, the movement for the complete emancipation of women, has begun to be conducted also in the family itself. A thorough knowledge of the ideological aspect of the movement for the complete emancipation of women and the growing power of seeing into the problem of emancipation of women on the part of communists and of all workers, are the surest warranty that the tasks outlined by the Party with regard to the problem of women will be successfully carried out.

The qualitative leap which is now met with in promoting the struggle for the emancipation of women is not casual. It has been prepared by the entire historical development of our country under the leadership of our Party of Labor, by the persistent and systematic struggle and work done by our Party for more than twenty-five years in succession for the emancipation of women, it is the result of the correct Marxist-Leninist line which our Party has pursued and keeps pursuing also towards the problem of women.

Right at the start of its very existence, our Party pointed out to the Albanian women, just as it pointed out to all the people, that the only way to their complete emancipation was for them to participate in the struggle waged by the people to put an end to all kinds of oppression and exploitation. And putting into practice this lesson of the Party and under its guidance, the women of our country took also active part in the liberation struggle, winning in this way their equal rights with men by shedding their blood. The mass heroism of women in the struggle for liberation, the names of Zoja Çurre, Bule Naipi, Margarita Tutulani, Liri Gerro, Shejnaze Juka, Qeriba Deri, Floresha Myteveliu, Bukurie Bazo, Pinelopi Pirro and many other women comrades who laid down their lives in the field of battle will be honored and will be remembered to the end of time not only for the great contribution they rendered to ensuring the freedom of people and laying the foundation to our People's Rule but also as outstanding pioneers and fighters for the emancipation of Albanian women.

After liberation, good results have been attained in the struggle for the complete emancipation of women thanks to the persevering efforts and concern of our Party and Comrade Enver Hoxha. In our socialist society women have not only been freed, like all our working people, from every class oppression and exploitation but they have won equal political rights and democratic freedoms with men sanctioned by law by our People's Power. They have won the right to elect and to be elected to all organs of government to as high a level as the People's Assembly, to take part in running the affairs of the country, in filling all state and social functions. Women take active part in all fields of social production in both rural and urban regions enjoying equal pay for equal work with men. They have become a major force in the struggle to complete the construction of socialism. The Party and People's Government have conferred the right to and created substantial opportunities for women to acquire education and culture, to raise their technological and professional capabilities which have made them capable of working and playing a leading role in all the sectors of people's economy and culture. During the years of People's Power a great change has been wrought in the Weltanschauung of Albanian women, their political awareness and ideological level have been enhanced. They are now an important factor in promoting the process of revolutionizing the whole life of the country. All this has raised the personality of women in our society and have made their role decisive in building socialism.

The magnitude of victories achieved by the Albanian women under conditions of People's Rule is more clearly seen if we keep in sight their deplorable state under former antipopular regimes which Comrade Enver Hoxha has pictured in these' terms: *"All the people used to suffer under bondage in the past but the Albanian women suffered most. They had to bear the whole weight of feudal and bourgeois laws which made real slaves of them. The canons of the Sharia and of the Church closely linked with the laws of the bourgeoisie considered women as chattels, as things which could be sold and bought by males, mercilessly exploited, not daring to open their mouth and express their opinions and whose only function was to bear children and toil day and night as slaves; just as the bourgeoisie had turned workers into their proletarians so had the old ruthless customs of the Sharia, of the Church, of feudalism and of bourgeoisie turned the women into the proletarians of their husbands."*

(From Comrade Enver Hoxha's speech at the 4th Congress of the Women's Union of

Albania, 1955)

These profound changes that have come about in the life of the women of our country could be achieved within a period of little more than two decades only in a socialist country like ours which is guided by a Marxist-Leninist party like ours. The revolution which has been effected in the status of women, the radical changes that have come about in their life, are a clear manifestation of the grandeur of the profound revolutionary changes that have taken place in all fields in our country. *"The development of a given historical epoch» Marx says «can always be gauged by the degree of progress of the women towards freedom... the level of emancipation of women represents the natural measure of total emancipation."* (Marx, Engels, Works, Russian edition, vol. II, page 224).

In spite of all these achievements, our Party is well aware that there is still a good deal to be done with regard to the problem of women. First of all, the whole of our society, including the women themselves, should get rid of all backward customs and mentality alien to our proletarian ideology and ethics which still exist among us and which lower the personality of women, smother and prevent them from developing their capabilities and their active participation in building the new life. With a view to achieving the complete emancipation of women so that they may fully enjoy in life equal rights with men, that they may occupy the place they deserve in our society and may properly play their major role, it is necessary to solve a series of other matters which deal with raising their participation at work, their promotion to posts of responsibility, their greater activization in the political and social life of the country, their educational and cultural uplift, their deliverance from household drudgery and with strengthening family ties on a sound socialist basis.

The struggle for the complete emancipation of women, to carry it through to the end is one of the fundamental and vital problems of furthering our revolution and completing the construction of socialist society. In the 1967 April 29 Statement of the Central Committee of the Party of Labor and the Council of Ministers of the People's Republic of Albania we read: *"No freedom of the people and of each individual, no progress of the country and achievement of our aims can he thought of without the complete emancipation of women."*

The problem of the complete emancipation of women is a broad and many-sided one requiring a number of measures of a political, educational, economic and administrative character to be taken for its solution. In this report we shall dwell mainly on the ideologic aspect of the problem of women because the solution of this problem involves a bitter ideological struggle between our Marxist-Leninist revolutionary socialist ideology and world outlook and alien, conservative and reactionary, feudal-bourgeois and patriarchal ideology and world outlook.

This struggle is one of the most complicated lines of march of our ideological revolution. This revolution has now burst forth with vehemence and is being conducted as a frontal attack against all forms of the ideology of the exploiting classes — bourgeois and revisionist, petty-bourgeois and conservative, feudal and patriarchal — against all impurities ranging from bourgeois individualism to the barbarous customs of enslavement and degradation of women. While being always on our guard against bourgeois and revisionist ideology which constitutes a danger not only to

17

the present but also to the future, our Party stresses also the need for an intensive fight against the most outworn reactionary forms of the ideology of the exploiting classes which are equally dangerous since they smother the revolutionary drive of workers and hamper them from taking active part in our struggle. It is within this framework that the fight is conducted for the all-round emancipation of women against old traditions, norms and customs which lie in the way of this emancipation.

It is part of the struggle to create the new man who is guided in life by communist ethics and norms, one of the requirements of which are to consider women as comrades and fellow fighters to build socialist society, a requirement that runs counter to the reactionary bourgeois ethics which legalizes the oppression and degradation of women just as it legalizes exploitation of the proletariat by capitalists. All denigrating concepts towards women which appear in various measures also among communists and cadres are offsprings and survivals of feudal religious and bourgeois ideology, therefore, alien and dangerous to our Marxist-Leninist ideology and to the cause of the socialist construction of our country. The struggle against them which lies at the root of the movements which have recently sprung up for the emancipation of women, is a major and long one which the Party should lead at this stage of development of our society.

In pursuance of the decisions of our 5th Party Congress and Comrade Enver Hoxha's February 6 speech, this plenum of the Central Committee of our Party should see to' it that the flames of the revolutionary movements be kept ablaze, that the torch which has been kindled be taken to the most remote corners of the country so that it may not only burn up everything that lies in the way of the complete emancipation of women but also to pave the way for the introduction of new norms, customs and traditions based on our communist ethics, so that the role and participation of women in the struggle to build socialism and communism may be further raised.

RAISE PARTICIPATION AND ACTIVITY OF WOMEN IN SOCIAL PRODUCTIVE WORK AND IN THE WHOLE POLITICAL AND SOCIAL LIFE OF THE COUNTRY

Our Party has consistently clung and clings to the Marxist-Leninist view that the broad participation of women in productive work and in the whole political and social life of the country is decisive for the complete emancipation of women and the promotion of revolution and socialist construction of our Fatherland.

1. On participation of women in social production

Work, social production is the basis of human existence and social development. In social work women attain their economic independence and real parity with man, it is at work that they assert their personality and are trained as social activists, that they acquire political awareness and revolutionary world outlook, that they get rid of backward prejudices and customs, that they are molded and educated as fellow members of socialist society. *"The factor work"*, comrade Enver Hoxha says, *"is a major factor for the economic, ideological and political emancipation of women. Toward this factor should we ever continually base our further efforts to do away with obstacles"*.

In line with this important principled thesis, our Party and government have always devoted special attention to the participation of women in production and have created all facilities for them to participate in an active way in social production.

After liberation this question was raised with special emphasis because of the utter economic and social backwardness our country had inherited from the past when the participation of women in productive work was very limited, in town and cities even unheard of. We had to start this work from almost nothing and overcome many obstacles and difficulties both in creating the necessary material conditions for the women to take part in production and also in eradicating fanaticism and old ideas, religious prejudices and backward customs which condemned women to stay within the four walls of their houses.

A radical change has been effected and a great victory has been won in this domain among us during the years of People's Power: over 248.000 women and girls take part now in production and this is 42% of the total number of urban and rural workers. With rare exceptions, we find the women engaged in all professions and branches of our people's economy while in some of these branches they make up the majority of workers as, for instance, in the textile industry 73%, in the food-processing industry 52%, in public health and sanitation 69.4% and so on. This has been a decisive step the Party has taken towards the emancipation of women, the importance of which is more clearly seen when we draw a comparison with some other states which have not experienced the utter backwardness which characterized our country 20 to 25 years ago. Thus, for instance, according to official statistical returns, the number of women workers in Jugoslavia in 1964 made up 29.3% of all workers, in Bulgaria — 34%, in Poland — 36%, in Rumania — 27.6%, in Italy — 22.9%, and in Greece — 27.8%.

Women in our country have become now such a great force that no 5-year plan can be fulfilled and no major economic and social mass action can be undertaken without their participation. In no job do they do less than men and in many cases, they work with a higher sense of duty, with more perseverance, with more attention to detail and with a higher sense of discipline than they.

In spite of this we should not arrive at the conclusion that the participation of women in productive work can now be considered as a problem which has been entirely solved in our country.

What problems emerge in this field? The first problem we have to tackle is that of getting all the women employed, for about 10% of them (in cities about 17%) do not yet take part in social work, this having negative consequences to the detriment of the life of women themselves and to the detriment of socialist construction. The main difficulty here is not the lack of work fronts, as some people claim. Our country is being rapidly transformed. Vast construction works are being set up everywhere demanding man power. Agriculture is another sector which stands in need of farmhands. Education, culture and science are continually developing not only in depth but also in breadth. Handicrafts and public services are expanding, therefore, there are work fronts in our country which stand always in need of workhands.

The question is that certain other reasons, mainly of a subjective character, reasons connected with certain wrong notions by many people have exerted their influence on preventing full participation of women at work. Thus, by viewing participation in work from a one-sided, individualistic angle, only dependent on the needs of the family budget, there are still women who do not take part in productive social work. There are even cases, both in the countryside and in cities, when husbands, not standing in need of the income of their wives have withdrawn them from work and confine them to household chores. This, of course, smacks of proprietorship, of petty bourgeois egoism which considers woman as the property of man and who' should do only household chores. There are also cases when, because of alien concepts about work, certain women in cities are shy of productive work where such work is needed, and run after "preferred jobs". In fact, this is an aristocratic attitude towards work incompatible with the ethical norms of our society. The Party should, fight against such concepts of those who connect the participation of women in work with their financial needs and personal comfort, entirely ignoring the fact that the mission of women as members of society is primarily to participate in social productive work for the socialist construction of the country.

These concepts do not only legalize the enslavement of women within the four walls of their homes but are very detrimental also to the general interest of socialist construction. It is a fact that the development of industry and of building construction in our cities has drawn and, in some cases, is still drawing workers away from the countryside. And this at a time when there are still unemployed city women and when the countryside itself stands in sore need of workhands. A tremendous gain would accrue to national economy if these jobs were filled by city women.

Backward customs to leave household chores to women and not to allow them to take part in social production cause great damage to the development of socialist economy in the countryside as well. Apart from the fact that about 8% of the women in the countryside do not participate at all in socialist production, the average number of workdays of women in all agricultural cooperatives Is lower than of men, while in many of them there are women who do not even reach the obligatory minimum of workdays. Thus, the average number of workdays by women throughout the Republic last year was 195 while that of men 294. About 1200 women in the Tepelena district failed to reach the minimum number of workdays. The same thing happened in the Gramshi district. It goes without saying that the overall participation of women and the increase of the number of workdays by them would go a long way to increasing social production and achieving their self-emancipation. In this respect, the Party organization and management of agricultural cooperatives in the countryside, particularly, in mountainous regions, should see to it that the women should continually increase their participation in work all the year round.

The rapid development of productive forces in our socialist society has deepened and widely specialized social division of labor, has created new branches and sub-branches of economy which create and can create many jobs for women. It must be said that, in spite of achievements attained, certain erroneous views prevent the women from embarking on a wider front of production. Thus, there prevails a striking conservatism among many cadres who hinder the participation of women in certain branches of social production claiming that there are no suitable jobs for women in them. This, in fact, narrows down in an artificial way the front of work for women. In the electric industry wo-r men make up only 13% of the number of workers, in that of machine making 19%, in building construction 10%, and so on. Can it be that there are jobs only for so many women in these sectors? Experience shows the contrary to be true. 400 women and girls passed through the school for training worker reserves and courses at the Tractor Machine Shop in Tirana and are now employed as workers turning out as much and ever more work than men. The fact that the number of women and girls employed at this plant make up 30.7%, while at the Machine Shop 54.6% of the total number of workers, refutes all pseudo-scientific "arguments" of these diehards and proves that women can and should work also in metal cutting machines, in repairing machinery and in every sector.

The view that jobs suitable for women are only those so called "light" or "clean"- ones is alien because of the very nature of our social order. It endorses the opinion of many men and many women that a women's profession is to sew, cook, do the cleaning, run creches and so on.

The struggle of the Party against a conservative attitude of discriminating jobs suitable to women in the various branches of economy, culture and administration should be one of the main directives to achieve the full participation of women in social work. Availabilities are at hand with us to expand the participation of women in the administration just as in the sectors of public health, trade and education in which many of the workers are women already. But greater availabilities exist, as we said, in other sectors of economy in which the participation of women is still on a limited scale.

While fighting against the conservative concepts and tendencies to draw a line between the professions of women and men the Party should also fight the other erroneous tendency to assign women to all kinds of jobs without taking into account their functions as mothers. Our socialist legislation protects women as workers and as mothers, therefore the organizations of the Party, of the Trade Unions and of the Union of Women should strive to protect women at work, to create most suitable conditions for the life and health of workers as mothers.

It is clear that in order to draw all the women into social productive work, the organizations of the Party and those of the masses should not stand aloof and should not be content only with the general percentage of participation of women in work. They should firmly fight against all alien concepts which prevent women from taking active part in work, should detect where they spring from and expose their reactionary bourgeois ideological nature. On the other hand, the problem of participation of women in production should become the object of special study for the state and economic organs concerned and, on the basis of this study, to establish the concrete steps which should be taken both to broaden the participation of women in work at the existing sectors as well as to open up new fronts of work. The experience gained during these recent months in the cities of Tirana, Shkodra and Durres where, under the sponsorship of the organs of the Party and Government, many new sectors of work have been created, clearly shows that there exist many opportunities for drawing as many women to work as possible.

An important problem that should draw the attention of the Party, of the trade Unions and of the State and economic organs is that of assigning more and more women to qualified jobs and to posts of responsibility. The Party has continually pointed out that this is not a simple but a principled problem emanating from a correct understanding of the place and role of women in socialist society, from the ability of the women themselves, their loyalty to the cause of the Party and people, qualities which are by no means less prevalent in women than in men.

The Party and State organs have continually worked in this direction and the results are good, bearing no comparison with the past. In centers of work and production there are thousands of women of high qualification employed as directresses of factories and combines, brigade leaders and manageresses of agricultural cooperatives, and so on. Following the 5th Party Congress and Comrade Enver Hoxha's February 6th speech this year, other special steps have been taken in Gjirokastra, Shkodra, Tirana, Burrel and elsewhere both to raise the qualification of women as well to promote them to posts of responsibility. Nevertheless, the situation in this direction cannot be considered satisfactory.

It is a fact that the overwhelming majority of women engage in simple unqualified work. This tendency is met with both in the countryside and in cities, both in economic enterprises and in the offices of the administration. Even in those branches of economy where participation of women is highest as, for instance, in the light and food — processing industries, in the woodworking and paper industries etc. the jobs requiring high or medium qualification, are occupied by men. The job of assistant manager in the textile industry, that of vacuum operator or presser in the food-processing industry, of superintendent of machinery and technology in the woodworking and paper industries have been monopolized by men although possibilities exist for them to be handled by women.

Still worse is the situation with regard to' promoting women to posts of responsibility. The number of women and girls in charge of brigades, of departments in factories, schools and other institutions is still quite small not to mention higher posts. Even in those sectors where the overwhelming majority of workers are women and girls, the posts of qualified work and responsibility are occupied by men. Thus, for instance, in the field of public health and sanitation, in which women make up about 69.4% of the total number of workers, of the 65 directors and assistant-directors of hospitals only 2 are women. In the sector of trade where women occupy 50.1% of the total number of workers, of the 207 directors and assistant directors only 13 are women. In the sector of education and culture, of the 325 workers of the ministry and regional sections of education only 26 are women.

Why are the Party organization and State and economic organs at the center and at the grassroots so hesitant in assigning women to qualified work and to posts of responsibility?

There is no doubt that one of the reasons is the low technological and educational level of the women themselves. We will take this up in more detail later on. But this is not the only and principal reason. For teachers and physicians, for instance, possess both vocational training and necessary cultural level, at least, equal to that of men and yet they are not appointed directors of schools or medical institutions, functionaries of responsibility in districts or at the center. These posts are preferably given to men. It is clear that the main obstacle in turning over qualified jobs to women or promoting them to posts of responsibility lies in "blemishes" inherited from the past, lies in conservative mentalities which have gripped also our leading cadres belittling women and lacking confidence in their efforts and capabilities. This is fundamental. The others like the women's own hesitancy, the tendency of some of them to shirk responsible jobs and to prefer simple ones, etc. are of secondary importance, and unfounded are claims that "women are overburdened with household chores" and should, therefore, not be assigned to leading posts, and so on.

Party committees, grass-root organizations and state organs, the comrades in charge of them should study this problem seriously, should repudiate every alien idea, should look ahead so that a turning point should be reached within a short time conformable with the wishes of the Party to assign women to jobs they are fit for. On the other hand, one should not lose sight of the negative experience of the past when women comrades promoted to positions of responsibility were not given any aid, technical or educational, when they were left to manage for themselves under the pressure of a conservative environment, especially in the countryside, instead of being seriously helped to overcome initial handicaps and do their job of responsibility, they were charged with and later dismissed as incapable for the job. An end should be put to such impermissible practice. The Party should continually strive not only to promote women to posts of responsibility but to see to it that they accomplish their jobs well and march always ahead.

2. On participation of women in the political and I social life of the country

The broad and effective participation of women in political and social life, in conducting class struggle, in directing the affairs of our state and society is the other decisive aspect of the complete emancipation of women, for it is a major school of the revolutionary education of women which awakens their ideological and political consciousness, making them aware of their great and , decisive role in society, giving them a chance to I get a thorough knowledge of the line of the Party, imbuing them with the revolutionary ideals of the Party, making them active fighters for their rights. In line with the teachings of Marxism-Leninism, our Party has always attached importance to drawing women to the political and social life of our country, considering this as one of decisive conditions both in the struggle for liberation as well as in socialist construction. J. V. Stalin has said: *"Women workers, urban and rural women workers are the greatest reserve of the working class. This reserve represents half of the population. On whether this reserve of women is with or against the working class depends the destiny of the proletarian movement, the triumph or defeat of proletarian revolution, the triumph or defeat of proletarian state powers."* (J.V. Stalin, Vol. 7, page 48, Albanian edition).

The women of our country are closely bound to the Party. In the Party they see their salvation from age-long and manyfold bondage, in the Party they see the mainspring of free and happy life for themselves and their children. Organized in the ranks of their organization, the Women's Union of Albania, or taking part as outstanding activists in the ranks of the Labor Youth Union, the Trade Unions or of the Democratic Front, the women of Albania strive with courage to build our socialist country and make it prosper. Participation of women in the whole political and social life of the country is today very broad and active: 40 women are representatives at the People's Assembly, 10,878 have been elected to people's councils, 1168 to people's tribunals, 30.088 women and young women take part in leading forums of mass organizations, over 8,280 women are members of our Party of Labor, 300,000 women are members of the Women's Union of Albania and about 82.000 young women of the Labor Youth Union of Albania.

There is no major Party or State problem in which the women do not have their say. They took active part in deliberations and drawing up the 4th five year plan, they have rendered a valuable contribution to the battle against bureaucratic manifestations and aberrations which our Party has embarked on with courage, they have put their heart and soul to the major battle our country is engaged in to uproot feudal and bourgeois ideology, they are working and striving like revolutionaries in all fields of socialist construction. The large scale activization of women in all revolutionary movements that have burst forth like a volcano in our country is a vivid proof of the enhancement of the political awareness of the women masses and a factor of primary importance in promoting these movements.

Love of country, of the Party and of socialism has been and is a distinctive feature of the Albanian women. They have always upheld and have courageously fought for the line of our Party. They have shown to be resolved fighters in the struggle against imperialists and Khrushchevite and Titoite revisionists, against deflectors and all enemies of our country. The question of defending the freedom and independence of our country has become the most dearly cherished cause of every woman.

Elections were held a few days ago to the organs of local administration and to people's tribunals. The fact that thousands of women were unanimously nominated and elected as people's representatives to people's councils and as judges, representing 36.17% of all elected representatives and 36% of judges, bespeaks not only the sympathy and confidence these activists have won among the laboring masses but it also shows the degree of the active participation of women in the political life of the country.

The great achievements attained in drawing the women to the political and social life of the country, which bear no comparison with the past when women were kept altogether out of every political and social activity, shows that, under conditions of proletarian dictatorship, the Party and People's Regime have raised the role of women to a level unknown to and unreached by even the so-called democratic bourgeois countries.

But judging the role of women as one of the most revolutionary forces of our society the Party lays down the task of urging the women to take more active part in all the fields of the political and social life of the country. We must not lose sight of the fact that in the matter of urging women to take more active part in political and social activities we have many flaws and deficiencies which become more apparent now when we are waging a campaign to further revolutionize the whole life of the country, when we are further deepening our revolution.

How can one speak of the emancipation of women and of urging them to take active part in the political and social life of the country when some bigoted men, particularly in the countryside, forbid women to take part in meetings and conferences, deny them the right of speech and pretend that they alone represent the village or work center? It is symptomatic that many young women members of the Labor Youth Union of Albania are very active and revolutionary as such but, once they are married, they turn into passive members of the organization, they cease to show the same verve and often are not even allowed by their husbands or their husbands' families to take part at the meetings of their organization. An equally disquieting fact too is the attitude of parents or husbands who falling victims to bigotry and gossip, do not allow their daughters or wives to participate in sports and physical culture, in artistic and cultural activities. And, what is worse, there are among us communists also who forbid their wives or sisters to take part in political and social life, who raise a hue and cry when their wives come late from meetings or who forbid their daughters to associate with their classmates or to take part in joint social work or mass actions of various kinds. Such conducts are altogether incompatible with the revolutionary features of a Party member.

This erroneous conduct has its source in the oppression and backwardness the women have been victims to through centuries, traces of which cannot be wiped out at once, for they spring from patriarchal and bourgeois concepts which have struck deep root in our minds and which constitute a backward world outlook influenced by the economic exploitation of women in the family, by feudal and bourgeois ethical norms and by the attitude of religion towards women. We should by all means uproot these alien concepts for they are at variance with the principles of our socialist democracy and deny to the women those political rights and prerogatives which our People's Power has guaranteed by law.

Socialist democracy cannot develop and the great principle of our Party on the line of the masses cannot be put into practice without the broad activization of the women masses, without soliciting their revolutionary creative thinking. The positive experience accumulated by many Party organizations, especially of late, indicates clearly that women, just as men, are capable of sizing up correctly the policy of the Party and government, that they present a bold front at discussions, advance remarks, suggestions and proposals about the work of economic enterprises and agricultural cooperatives, about the activities of the organs of administration and of the masses where they militate. Therefore, it is essential that special concern should be devoted to the question of soliciting the opinion of women and that of cultivating their political awareness not only by the organizations of the Women's Union of Albania, as it often happens in practice, but also by all the organizations of the Party and of the masses as well. A great deal of work of agitation should be done with men, in the first place, but also with women as well. One should fight against such reactionary ideas as "politics is not within the scope of women", against fanatical suspicions that participation of girls and women at meetings or mass actions impairs their honor; an end should be put to a state of affairs in which the women, especially in the countryside, are under the constant pressure of the conservative opinion which ignores the say and opinion of women on political and social matters. It should be clear to the organizations of the Party and of the masses that the better informed the women are and the more they participate in directing and solving political, economic and social problems the more democratic will our People's Regime become.

Another important aspect of the participation of women in political and social activity is their participation in problems dealing with the organization and management of production. The Party has constantly stressed the need for strengthening socialist democracy, especially in agricultural cooperatives. This is of major importance also to state economic enterprises. Since women make up a great force in production, nearly half of the member of workers, their aid and contribution is considerably large. Therefore, Party organizations and economic organs should devote special attention to soliciting the creative thought of women in this respect, to getting more of them participate in various committees like that of planning, of social control, etc. This will strengthen our democracy and will help socialist economy to develop in the right way and with success, it will raise the role of women in the problems of the economic life of the country.

Of major importance is also the active and broad participation, especially, of young women in the cultural artistic and physical cultural life of the country. In this field we should strive in two main directions. On one hand, we should see to it that women may have their say and take active part in creating and developing our national culture and art. On the other, we should see to it that women may draw as much profit as possible from all the cultural, artistic and physical cultural activities which take place in our country. In this respect, a campaign should be waged both against trends that underrate and belittle the creative ability of women as well as against the bigotry and derogatory attitude that certain men maintain who, in fact, deprive women of all possibility to read, to frequent the theater, movies and other activities, to engage in sports and physical culture, considering these as the privileges of men alone.

Our attention should especially be drawn to the participation of women in the ranks of the Party. Their number has been grown from one year to another. This is a positive thing. Especially of late the Party organizations have been doing better in this direction. Thus, for instance, as from January this year the number of women newly admitted to membership in the Party has been 30 in the district of Gjinokastra, 22 in that of Berat, 14 in the Shkodra district and so on. Nevertheless, if we study figures carefully, it turns out that the number of women Party members is still small, making up only 12.4% of the entire roll-call of the Party. Why does this happen? This is first and foremost, the result of lack of confidence in the capabilities of women which has struck root also in the Party organizations. It reflects the extremely unsatisfactory work done by the Party organizations with women. How else can one account for the fact that in certain work centers as at the "Stalin" Textile Mills where, although most of the workers are women there are twice as many men in the Party ranks as women, or at all the organizations of the Kukes district which have admitted only 54 women to Party membership since the liberation of the country to this day, or that of the Librazhdi district which has admitted only one woman to membership during the whole of 1966, etc.

The Party committees and organizations usually justify themselves for few admittances of women to Party membership by claiming that the ideological and political level and their cultural training is still low. But who is to blame for this? Does this not reflect the insufficient work done by the Party organizations to train women for the Party? It is, therefore, essential for the Party organizations lo radically improve their method of political and educational work with women and, at the same time, to wage a resolute campaign against the conservative and backward ideas which some communists cherish about the alleged incapability of women.

If we hurl away the conservative concepts which underrate the ability of women to be in the ranks of the Party we will tear up the veil covering our eyes and will see women as they truly are: as capable champions of the cause of the Party, as great a revolutionary force as men. In certain aspects of life they are even more revolutionary and better aware of carrying out the line of the Party than men. The conscience of a woman is unstained for she has never oppressed nor ruled but has always sacrificed herself for the happiness of others. Speculation and nepotism are alien to her. From this point of view swelling the Party ranks with women comrades will invigorate the life of the grass-root organizations, will raise their combative ability and will strengthen the unity of the ranks of the Party. Therefore, it is the primary duty of all Party organization to try to find, activate and train the most deserving women to become members of our Party without in any way affecting the requirements for admission to Party membership. The women and girls themselves should, at the same time, consider their admittance to Party membership as a very important problem. The present marvellous revolutionary movements which have been spread throughout the country and which have widely gripped and are daily gripping women and girls constitute a very good basis to step up the process of swelling the ranks of the Party with women comrades.

3. On the uplift of the cultural, educational, technical and professional level of women

One of the most important links in the struggle for the complete emancipation of women and especially, for their participation in qualified work, for their promotion to posts of responsibility or for their political and social activity is the uplift of their educational, cultural, technical and professional level. In contrast with the past, stupendous changes have been brought about in these fields too thanks to the concern of the Party and People's Rule. Among women, over 90% of whom were illiterate before liberation, illiteracy has been wiped out almost entirely up to forty years of age. All girls receive compulsory primary and 8 grade education. A good number of women and girls pursue their studies in secondary, vocational and higher day schools and those of the night and correspondence system. In comparison with 1960, the number of girls attending 8th grade and secondary schools has been doubled whereas in higher institutes of learning it is two and one-half times as high. Over 9,500 women and girls of secondary technical training and over 1,300 others of higher training are employed in various economic and cultural depart- merits. Today, our enterprises and institutions employ more women engineers than the total number of engineers Albania had before liberation and two and one-half times as many women physicians as the total number of physicians Albania had before liberation.

Despite this, the educational level of women as a whole is still low. This situation is connected with the backwardness and darkness which were the lot of women in the past. But this is not the only reason, for even during these years after liberation when the doors of schools were also opened to girls, when the education and culture of the people received special attention as a primary factor for the progress of the country, the rate at which women acquired technological and professional skill has been and continues to be lower than that of men. Why has such a thing happened? Among us there exist no privileges for men and no limitations for women in any field of education. Girls and women, just as everybody else in our country are eager to acquire knowledge and education, although, especially women and girl workers should exert more efforts to raise their political educational and technological professional level. Thus, there have been no specific objective reasons, at least during these recent years to account for the deficiencies noted in the educational and professional uplift of women. From a concrete analysis of facts, it turns out that the main obstacle to the progress of women lies in the retrogressive ideas prevailing about women, underrating their creative abilities. These ideas are manifested in various forms.

In the first place, many parents and husbands, especially in the countryside, hold the opinion that "girls have no. need of schooling", that "girls belong to others". Consequently, they do not only fail to follow up their progress at primary and 8-grade schools, which they are obliged by law to do, but they even withdraw them from school altogether under the pretext that they have grown up. Higher education is altogether out of the question for these girls. Thus, many young girls receive only primary school education which, in the long run, turns them into semi-illiterates if not illiterates in the full sense of the word. There are about 15,000 such women under the age of 40. Without in any case belittling the responsibility of the parents and husbands of these girls and women, it is clear that neither the organs of people's education nor the organizations of the Party and of the masses can be exempted from responsibility for this unfortunate situation. Their duty is not merely to point out this sad fact, but to take special educative and organizational steps, so that these girls and women are taught, that illiteracy is wiped out and, in the future not to allow any child, particularly girls, break off grade schooling which is compulsory by law.

But this is not the only consequence of alien ideas, the fact that women are looked down upon, that the problem of their qualification and enhancement of their cultural standard is not rightly understood, can be seen also in connection with the training of cadres. It is a commendable fact that 13% of the total number of cadres of higher training and 37% of cadres of medium training are women. But there has been room for higher percentages. Up to now the number of cadres trained in schools, technicums and courses of agricultural cooperatives has reached 13,000 of whom only 415 are women. Or of the 682 students pursuing their higher studies in the Agricultural College only 24 are girls while of the 332 students receiving instruction in farm Mechanics only 2 are girls. Do these figures alone not indicate the lack of interest on the part of the Ministry of Agriculture and of the regional Party committees to train cadres from the ranks of women? A more or less similar situation exists in other sectors. During the 1961-65 five-year period the higher institutes of learning including the 2-year Teacher Training Institutes turned out about 6,400 cadres. Only 1220 of them were girls. Technicums turned out 7,865 graduates of whom only 1,435 were young women. In the same way 12th grade schools turned out 7,700 graduates of whom only 27 were girls, while of the 10,850 students that graduated from lower vocational schools only 2,600 were girls. Nor should we feel content that there are today enrolled in the State University and in other institutes of learning 1,750 young women out of about 7,450 undergraduates and in secondary technical and professional schools there are 3,400 girls out of a total of 11,300 students. These figures indicate the lack of interest of both the central organs and Party Committees for the educational training of women and girls, they indicate the insufficient efforts exerted in breaking down all obstacles lying in the way of endowing women and girls with education and culture.

State organs and Party committees should put an immediate end to this situation. They should give priority to sending girls to professional and high schools with a view to raising their number much higher than up to now. In awarding scholarships too priority should be given to girls, especially from the countryside.

Insufficient concern about raising the cultural, technological and professional level of women is also evident as far as pursuance of night schools and organization of courses of qualification for women and young women workers goes. It must be avowed that the concern of the Party committees, the trade unions and economic organs in this regard has been quite insufficient. How else, can one account for the fact that the number of women and girls who attend 8 grade night schools, especially, these recent years has been on the decline. Today the number of women and girls attending 8 grade night schools is only 1,370 while in 1960 their number was 3,000. Of course, the blame here lies also on the women and girls who have left school but what have the Party organizations, those of the masses and economic organs done to induce, to persuade them not to abandon school?

As far as qualification of women as the only way to assign them to qualified jobs and posts of responsibility is concerned the work of the economic organs and Trade Unions is unsatisfactory. Of all qualified women workers, women make up 25% while of approximately 14.700 qualified women only about 2.100 possess 6th category and above. The organizations of the Party, those of the masses and state organs should be earnestly concerned about this problem bearing in mind not only to open courses of qualification for women but to create suitable condition for these courses to be attended by the women, who while being workers are at the same time mothers as well.

Through persistent efforts by the Party and organizations of the masses, through harder work by the women and girls themselves and through the above technical and organizational measures we will succeed, in a relatively short period of time, in overcoming the striking disproportion existing today between the low level of qualification of women and the demands of advanced technique for higher qualification. This will help to solve more easily also the contradiction existing between the decisive role the women play as a major revolutionary force and as half of the population in socialist construction and their very insufficient mobilization for work of leadership in all phases of life.

* * *

A broader participation of women in production and in the political, social and cultural life of the country is the main road towards the complete emancipation, of women, this major force of our revolution and socialist construction. The general conclusion to be drawn from all this is that the root of all evil and main obstacle to the emancipation of women in our socialist society lie in the alien concepts about women which are deep rooted in the mentality of men and, to a large extent, in that of women themselves. According to these concepts, women are considered as inferior beings destined to serve men, to give birth to and bring up children, to do house chores, incapable of taking part on a basis of parity with men in social life, to create, to master culture, science and technological skill, and so on. It is essential to bring home to every communist, to every cadre and to every worker that these alien concepts have no, or nearly no material basis in our socialist society, that they are utterly at variance with our socialist reality, that they are gloomy survivals of the past in the conscience of people, that they are utterly incompatible with the principles of Marxism-Leninism, with the line and policy of our Party and our People's Rule and cause incalculable damage to the cause of our revolution and socialist construction. Without uprooting these concepts to the letter there can be no question of total emancipation of women and of completing the construction of socialist society. It is only when this problem is viewed in this way that the complete emancipation of women, making them co-partners in our society, will take the right course and be crowned with success.

CARRY TO THE END THE CAMPAIGN TO DELIVER THE WOMEN FROM THE DRUDGERY OF HOUSEHOLD CHORES

Strengthen and Promote Socialist Relations in the Family

The complete emancipation of women, their participation in productive work and in political and social life depend, to a large extent, on the establishment of the new socialist relations in the family, or the complete deliverance of women from the drudgery of household chores and from the survivals of feudal and patriarchal ethics on the attitude towards women.

The establishment of socialist relations in production, abolition of the exploiting classes and relations of private ownership, dissolution of patriarchal families in the countryside, participation of women in social production, transformations in the domain of the ideology and psychology of the urban and rural masses, have shaken the old relations between husband and wife to their very foundations, they have introduced in them many new socialist elements which have strengthened and developed the Albanian family on sounder foundations. Transformations in this field are under way and they are developing both in breadth as well as in depth. Socialist transformations are proceeding faster in urban families and slower in those of the countryside, especially in the remote mountain regions.

The process of uprooting old relations and establishing new socialist ones in the family cannot be wound up all at once, because, being complex and many-sided social relations, they are linked not only with transformation in the sphere of the material life of society, but have a direct bearing also on the various forms of social awareness: on ideology, politics, ethics and religion, psychology, the many and varied customs which have assumed the force of unwritten laws and which exert a major conservative resistance which have been preserved, are preserved and passed as a heritage from one generation to another. Therefore, transformations in the field of family relations, setting up new socialist relations, require a long, persistent and all-round battle, on a complicated and difficult field, against the ideology, psychology, ethics and customs inherited from the old society.

1) Uproot old marital relations that obstruct the complete emancipation of women and the establishment of the new socialist family.

Now more than ever one witnesses the new phenomena which are developing and taking a solid shape in the creation of the new family as a result of the many years of work the Party has been doing with the masses on concluding marriages on new socialist foundations and of the campaign against old and reactionary customs regarding this question.

What is new in this lies in the fact that the young man and young woman, while working or attending school together, have better opportunities to get acquainted with, sympathize and love each other, get the consent of their families and join in wedlock. In other cases, when they do not work together or when they have had no opportunity to get acquainted with each other, as it occurs in certain agricultural cooperatives or villages, cases are not rare when, especially the mother, asks her daughter and gets her consent to marry. Now and more so every day in picking a bride or a bridegroom people give no longer preference to "rank", to the past economic and social standing of the family as they used to do before, but to the good conduct of the young woman and young men. Cases are becoming more and more frequent when religious and other differences are no longer considered an obstacle to conclusions of marriages by either the young women and young men themselves or by their parents.

What is of primary importance is that more and more conditions are being created to proceed along this line. The movements that Comrade Enver Hoxha's call on February 6 this year sparked off throughout the country in defense of the rights of women and girls aim, first and foremost, at setting up new marital relations, at further strengthening our socialist family. Men and women have raised their voice against and condemn with indignation the ugly custom of betrothal of children, of marriages between persons of big differences in age, of selling off girls in marriage and of treating women as the last ranking person in the family. Hundreds of betrothals, which had been concluded on unjust criteria have been dissolved as a consequence of this campaign and many people have pledged themselves to do away with all backward customs that trampled underfoot the freedom and dignity of women.

The Party organizations in many districts, especially in those of Mirdita, Mati, Shkodra, Tropoja, Tirana, Fieri, have succeeded in conducting an important campaign correctly by setting in motion people of all walks of life, men and women, old and young. This campaign should be kept up and taken through to the end. The Party organizations should not be content with the results achieved and obligations that have been pledged, because the old is deep rooted, is very conservative and, if it is not fought with consistency and in a systematic way, through persistent educative work, it may come back into force again.

The struggle in defense of the rights of women and girls especially, as regards correct marital relations, should be firmly waged not only in the countryside, but also in the cities, because there exist here also backward and feudal customs and concepts, which, are intertwined with other bourgeois and petty bourgeois opinions. These are manifested in the endeavors of some conservative parents to pick husbands for their daughters mainly according to their social "rank", to their economic standing, to their "preferable" profession even according to their place of abode, and not according to the moral,' qualities of the grooms to be, they are manifested in the tendency of some parents to betroth their daughters, while they are still too young "lest they lose their reputation" resulting from gossip that may spread because of their associating with boys at work, at school, at various social gatherings, sport, artistic and other activities. Some young men and young women themselves are not exempt from such opinions on betrothal.

The organizations of the Party and those of the masses, particularly those of youth and women, should do more intensive educative work in order to create a new world outlook, the communist world outlook, about contracting marriages. Communist parents themselves should set an example in this direction. The youth organization is expected to do better work in this direction. As in all problems, in this too, which is directly connected with their own life, the young men and young women should be unflinching fighters for the establishment of communist ethical standards. They should wage a particular campaign against gossip, against all the people, even the young, who indulge in gossip, who blabber here and there trying to stain sincere friendship, sound comradeship, the moral attributes of our young men and young women. The Party has stressed time and again that in the campaign against backward customs, which trample upon the dignity of girls and women, the source of evil is not to be looked for simply in the "ruthless conduct" of this or that father, brother or husband, but one should delve deeper into the problem of why, how and where' these age long customs are kept alive. Many of the customs, which at our time are considered barbarous and inhumane, spring from other factors, such as the problem^ of establishing connections and concluding alliances between clans, that of dire poverty and anxiety of parents to provide dresses for their daughters, and so on. A deep insight into customs and their origin, into their blending with religious beliefs, prejudices etc. will enable the Party organizations to undertake a more fruitful campaign to persuade people, and even the most backward, of the futility of these customs and of the necessity of doing away with them in our days.

The problem of women, therefore, and the problem of strengthening the new family, *"is not a problem that can be solved within one year"*, Comrade Enver Hoxha has said, *"This is a perpetual problem, the solution of which requires long stages, each of which has its own various problems of development of quality. Each generation has its own problems. Old concepts disappear, new ones take shape. And it is precisely this development we do not intend to leave to spontaneity, we guide it with much ado and in the direction we desire."* Our Party has treated and treats the problem of creating the new family with heedful concern, it is guided by Marxist-Leninist teachings, according to which new society cannot be built without establishing new socialist relations in the family too, between husband and wife and among other members, that the sounder and cleaner the family the much stronger is socialist society itself.

Mutual acquaintance, unstained and sincere friendship established at work and in the common struggle of the young man and young woman should be at the root of the new family of our society. Marriage is a matter which is primarily their concern and they should not reconcile themselves with what is conservative and reactionary, they should be on the forefront of battle for what is new. But the parents cannot stand aloof and not exert their influence on such an important problem of life as that of the marriage of their offspring. They possess the experience of life, the revolutionary spirit gained in life and struggle but together with these parents are often conservative and inherit many concepts and stigma of alien ideology and morals from old society. Therefore, they should analyze their own experience in the spirit of criticism, they should judge with calm' wisdom, they should study and try to understand the new objective and subjective conditions which have been created, the aspirations, sentiments of what is new and the revolutionary impulse of youth.

The Party and organizations of the masses should conduct more intensive, intelligent and all-round work with the masses of youth and young pioneers with a view to imbuing them with the sense of the progressive new, with a correct understanding of love and of the family. Young men and young women, imbued with communist morals by the Party, should fight against any alien manifestation in relations among them which relations should be characterized by a sound social spirit with sentiments of mutual respect and solidarity running through them.

The establishment of the new family cannot be effected without doing away the ugly custom, of dowries as one of the open manifestations of marital relations based on relations of private ownership and a moderate variation of the customs of selling off and buying girls which is preserved to this day in all the urban and rural regions of our country. The organizations of the Party and those of the masses should give full support to the revolutionary initiatives taken by the people at meetings of the Democratic Front to put an end to these mediaeval customs of grave consequences to the relations between husband and wife and to the economy of each family and they should conduct broad clarifying discussions with workers on this topic.

Dowry should not be confused with the concern of parents to come to the aid of their children, with their concern to come to their aid within their available means to help them establish their new home. Parents should, above all, endow their children with the qualities of communist ethics so that they may be able to found a sound family, built by the joint efforts and contributions of both the bride and the groom and not by the dowry.

A determined fight should be waged also against certain other customs at work on the wedding day of the bride, which are intended to legalize the submission of the wife to her husband. Such are, for instance, the insolent ceremony in receiving the bride into the groom's house as well as the ceremony of a religious character which sanctifies relations of oppression and exploitation. In Christ's name, the priest sanctified the wedlock of an aged man with a young woman in her teens. While the hoxha, holding the Koran in his hand, blessed the wedding of a man to his fourth wife: Both of them advised the wife in the name of religion to submit to the husband for he is her lord and master.

While fighting backward customs regarding the wedding ceremonies we must legalize our new customs of socialist society. This implies that we should view all ceremonies connected with marriage with a critical eye so as to preserve what is good and give it a new content and to discard what is negative by creating new traditions both as regards the ceremonies of marriages at the Registrar's Office and as regards wedding parties as an event of rejoicing avoiding feasts involving large and useless expenses.

2. Establishment of correct relations between

husband and wife and between the wife and other members of the family — an essential condition to entitle the wife to the place belonging to her in the family.

Setting up the new socialist family, in addition to founding on correct marital relations, requires also the establishment of truly equal relations between the wife, husband and other members of the family. It is a fact that in many families both in the countryside and in cities and even in certain cases, when marriages have been concluded on sound foundations, there exist and are kept intact many survivals of feudal-bourgeois practices, inherited from one generation to another, backward concepts and religious norms which have assumed the force of custom and law and which stifle and enslave the woman in the family.

In spite of their participation in production and the contribution the women render through their work, they do not yet occupy an equal post in the family, especially in the countryside. There still prevails the opinion that "man is the master of the house", "the head of the family", there still prevails the complete submission of the wife to the husband, the denial of her most elementary rights, which is legalized also by religion and the "Holy" scriptures.

At the numerous meetings and consultations which took place these recent months throughout the country the people themselves firmly condemned these ideas and all their burdensome consequences weighing upon wives who are assigned to the most menial and humiliating jobs in the family. Her lot is the lash rope, she must wash the feet of her husband and of all the other members of the family, she must be the first to get up in the morning and the last to go to bed at night, she must eat after they have had their meals, to carry wood, to haul water and so on. Can one speak of parity and of a sound family under such circumstances? These ugly customs do not prevail only in the countryside but also, in one measure or another, in cities where, in many cases the woman is not treated as an equal but a being of secondary importance.

The social and economic basis under which these concepts thrived has totally changed. In our country the rights of women are guaranteed by law also in this respect. But the force of habit is a ponderable one smothering both the men and other members of the family as well as the women on whom these habits and customs weigh.

Let us take up for instance, the Canon of Lek Dukagjini and view it from this angle. It reflects a social order based on the patriarchal and feudal system of clans and tribes and, for that reason, it embodies the patriarchal and feudal ideology. As concerns the attitude towards women, it contains the most enthralling, most humiliating and most ruthless norms that can be imagined. The material and general social conditions under which this Canon has sprung and which it reflects have, of course, radically changed. But the force of its ideology, the force of tradition and of customs still remain and, in certain regions, even prevail crippling and maiming the life of women. Is it not high time for us to uproot at once and bum at the stakes all these savage and barbarous traditions and customs?

Or, let us view the discontinuance of the lash rope from this angle. When this initiative was first taken at the "Asim Zeneli" agricultural cooperative in Gjirokastra certain old women said to the younger women and girls: "Well, never mind if you come back without a load on your back but, in any way, take the lash rope with you. It is unbecoming for a woman to go without her lash rope!" Here is a case renouncing "the economic advantage" accruing from this custom but holding fast to it as a symbol, as a sign of the bondage and humiliation of the woman, as a sign of her treatment as a beast of burden. And this custom was so strong that the lash rope was part of a bride's trousseau.

Therefore, we should declare a merciless war on all old reactionary customs that are based on the force and inertia of tradition. That is why the organizations of the Party and those of the masses, public opinion as a whole should combat with courage and without respite to uproot the psychology and old customs that degrade women and weaken our family. While intensifying their ideologic and clarifying work the organizations of the Party and those of the masses should support and encourage to the best of their ability all movements and the many obligations taken at meetings and consultations with regard to respecting the rights of women as a decisive condition for a sound family.

The women themselves should fight with courage to win equal rights with men in the family. They should not keep quiet and yield obeisance to these ugly customs allegedly for the sake of preserving harmony and unity in the" family. Harmony and unity in the family are basic elements for good marital relations but they are not strengthened by succumbing to prejudices and backward customs of subserviency to man but by fighting them in the right way with courage and wisdom. Silence and submission of women have their source especially in the idea that "the husband has you in his grip", he may divorce you and turn you back to your parent's house. Formerly, it was out of fear of being turned out of her husband's house and of being pointed to as a divorcee that she tolerated to share her husband's house with his second wife. Today, being economically as independent as her husband, she is master of her own, capable of bringing up her children and is not intimidated by the threat of divorce when living together becomes unbearable. Divorce is an equal right of both husband and wife and, if this right is correctly understood, it will not hang over the wife like the sword of Damocles as before, but will help strengthen family ites. The couple should exercise just as much discretion and wisdom when contemplating divorce as they exercised before they joined in wedlock. Public opinion condemns any rash gesture which wrecks the family and affects especially the children from whichever part it comes. The force of public opinion was manifested especially in the revolutionary situation which characterizes the life of our country at present.

A negative influence in preserving the backward customs in the life of many of our families is exerted by people advanced in age, the old men in particular, who, being victims of the force of habit and unconscious of the damage they do, insist that the members of the family should respect the customs. This handicap should be overcome with tact and not in open opposition which is liable to create conflicts as some young men and young women do, but by relying on the correct line of the Party, by working patiently with the old generation, by treating them with highest consideration, confident they will gradually and eventually give up their conservative views.

The organizations of the Party and those of the masses should do a great deal to point out the major right the women have won in the People's Regime, the importance of establishing correct relations between the wife and husband and all the other members of the family as an important factor for consolidating the family which should be based on the equality of husband and wife, on respecting the personality of each, on their equal rights and not on moldy, reactionary and conservative thought of patriarchal, feudal and bourgeois families.

They should strive, at the same time, to uproot the survivals of religious, feudal and patriarchal ethics on the attitude towards women and should see to it that the moral requirements of public opinion should be equal for both the women and men, that integrity and honor, fidelity in marital relations, freedom to choose life companions should be considered and be in practice the just rights of both the husband and his wife. We should in no way tolerate that social opinion should, allegedly in the name of proletarian ethics and of the sound traditions of honor and marital integrity of our people, treat and solve these problems falling victims to the laws and usages of the Church or of the Sharia, to the norms of religious, feudal and patriarchal morals, which in every case and always throw the blame • on and condemn the women. It is precisely these concepts and customs which prompt many parents and public opinion in general to frown upon the association of a young man with a young woman, the love' that may develop between them and which encourage gossip which, as a rule, weighs heavy upon the young woman, affects her dignity and personality. It must be brought home to everyone that without making both men and women morally equal there can be no genuine and all-round emancipation of women.

Problems of the family and family relations are not only a private concern of each but they are problems of society as a whole. Our socialist society is vitally concerned for the consolidation of the family on sound communist morals, for the family is the cell of society. The concept of viewing problems of the family as a private affair has brought about a feeling of unconcern about the conduct of people in the family, a kind of separate assessment of the moral and political make up of one or of the other from his conduct in the family and in society. This accounts for the fact that up to now in our society some workers and even communists and cadres who are resolved followers of the line of the Party, hard workers and endowed with a high spirit of sacrifice and self-denial, when in the family allow themselves behavior and acts which are incompatible with communist ethics. This accounts also for the fact that often even Party organizations in the countryside have maintained a lenient attitude towards alien patriarchal and bourgeois manifestations and have failed to mobilize public opinion to fight these manifestations with might and main.

The Party should fight equally against indifference and against vulgar intrusion into family affairs. The intimate, delicate and complicated nature of family relations should always be kept in mind in the work of Party organizations and workers' collectives. Society, the collective and everybody may exert a positive influence on strengthening the unity of the family only when this intervention is performed with tact and good judgment prompted by the sentiments of respect and social concern and not by resorting to administrative methods, methods of dictation, of pressure and of coercion. The intervention of others in every detail of family relations, for every problem that might arise in the family often does more bad than good, instead of exerting a positive influence in consolidating the family does the contrary and leads to weakening and even to breaking it up. Just as dangerous are ill intentioned gossip and sensational assertions which lead to discrediting the wife or husband before public opinion. Public opinion can never be indifferent towards and not pass harsh judgment on such amateurs and not counteract their negative influence on family relations.

Towards anti-social phenomena which are manifested in family relations, be they on the part of the husband, wife, parents or children, it is not only public opinion that acts and should act but also state organs, especially, the organs of justice and our legislation.

Our legislation on the family has played a major role in setting up socialist relations in the family, especially, in freeing the woman from drudgery and in securing her equality with man. But considering the new conditions that have been created, the revolutionizing spirit of the whole life of the country and the tasks the Party has outlined to further deepen revolution, the organs of justice should intervene more actively and be more skillful in protecting the rights of women and the norms of communist morals in family relations. On the other hand, in conformity with these conditions and this revolutionary spirit, they should re-examine with a critic's eye certain legal dispositions which govern family relations and which are outworn and do not reflect as they should the socialist transformations which have taken place in our country.

It is only when coordinated work is done by all the organizations of the masses, state organs and the various cultural and educational institutions under the leadership of the Party organizations, when educative and differentiated work is done with men and women, old and young and even children that socialist public opinion and psychology can be formed, that negative phenomena and outworn customs and mentality in family relations can be discarded and, on this basis, our family can always wax strong.

3. Free women from the drudgery of house chores

With a view to carrying the process of the complete emancipation of women further ahead and to achieve the equality of women with men, the attention of the Party should be concentrated, now and for long time to come, on the struggle to uproot all concepts and customs which treat women as slaves of the household, to free them from the drudgery of household chores. Lenin says: *"The woman continues to remain a household slave regardless of all laws passed to free her since she is oppressed, smothered, stifled and humiliated by the small-scale domestic economy which nails her down to the kitchen and to children, robbing her of her exertion for ruthlessly unproductive and grinding toil which shatters her nerves, benumbs her intellect and exhausts her altogether."*

The complete and ultimate deliverance

of women from the drudgery of household chores, of course, demands, as Engels has pointed out, the collectivization of this domestic economy, turning it into a branch of social production. This collectivization of domestic economy in the countryside and even in cities, however, does not depend entirely on our wishes and our will. In the countryside especially this process is a very complicated one. It requires a large-scale development of present technique and its own material and technical basis, it requires the collectivization of all service work in the family, it demands, in short, the liberation of the family from its functions as an economic unity.

But we cannot wait until the collectivization of domestic economy is fully achieved for freeing the women from the drudgery of the household. We should start right away to work in this direction with the means available now and with those which will be created step by step.

Thanks to the concern of the Party and of the organs of the People's Rule, a series of important steps have already been taken to shorten the time necessary for the daily chores of the household, for rearing and bringing up children and so on. Creches and kindergartens have been set in cities. Such institutions have also been set up in a certain number of villages, particularly during the period of intensive agricultural work. The network of public health service free of charge iri urban and rural centers has been extended. The network of trade units has been expanded and has been extended even to the remotest parts of the country; centers of handicraft service have been set up not only in the various city quarters but are being set up also in several villages. Popular restaurants have been opened in city quarters, the market has been flooded with ready-made garments for all ages, home-made pieces of furniture, household utensils brought also from abroad for laundry purposes, for cooking, house-cleaning and so on.

At present, two are the main ways to solve the problem of stepping up the process which has already begun in our country to free the women, to create possibilities for them to have more time available to devote to their educational, cultural and professional uplift and recreation;

Firstly, to strive to uproot concepts and customs which consider household work and the rearing of children as the job of women alone. It must be borne in mind that the women workers today after their day's work in factories, in fields or in offices have a second day's job to tackle at home cooking, cleaning, serving for all the members of the family and bringing up and educating children. In the countryside they have additional jobs to do: carrying wood and hauling water, kneading and baking bread. It can very well be said that a woman's workday lasts 15 to 16 hours. It is precisely on this account that every husband should seriously think out ways of helping his wife, his life companion.

The idea that men cannot and do not know how to do certain household chores is wrong and patriarchal. With the exception of a mother's function to take care of her youngsters, a man can very well take a hand in all the other chores of the household. This requires that men should cast off such concepts as that of being "ashamed" of doing kitchen work, house repairs, cleaning and ironing, that of keeping and educating children, hauling water and so on and so forth, making it a major problem for all public opinion and fighting against the force of habit which is a great stumbling block not only for men but also for women, especially those advanced in age.

The idea and psychology that household chores should not be confined only to women but to all the members of the family including men should be inculcated deep into children by the family, the school and society. This objective is not attained if the family keeps drawing a line, as it does today between jobs to be done by girls and those to be done by boys: girls to do the cleaning and putting the house in order, to learn cooking, sewing and embroidery, whereas boys only to chop wood, do the marketing and, in general, to do those jobs their father does. Such a division of "jobs for girls" and "jobs for boys" should not be made in schools and in various mass actions of youth, in pioneer homes, creches and kindergartens either. The Ministry of Education and Culture should reexamine and revise its programs of study connected with work and domestic economy so that no discrimination may be made between boys and girls.

Secondly, lighten a woman's household chores by expanding the network of public service and making a more efficient use of the existing one.

First of all, it is necessary to create further conditions to lighten the work of women as far as bringing up and educating children is concerned. The Political Bureau calls on the Council of Ministers to take immediate steps to increase the capacity of kindergartens and creches above plan on the basis of decisions taken about the use of funds accumulated as a result of the initiative taken by workers to give up voluntarily certain kinds of supplementary payments.

As concerns the long established agricultural cooperatives and those in lowlands, the Political Bureau calls on every cooperative to make full use of their availabilities and set up, mainly in brigades, either permanent creches and kindergartens or during the big campaigns of farm work. This should be of great assistance to mothers and a measure of major importance for the correct upbringing and education of children.

With a view to shortening the necessary time for household chores, state organs should study the ways of taking other measures.

The organs of industry, handicrafts and trade may turn out and put out the market larger quantities of house utensils and other more economical means for cooking, cleaning and laundry purposes. Trade organs should expand the varieties of packaged and dried food products and should study the possibility of organizing the sale of foodstuffs on order, as practiced in Tirana and Durres, for the distribution of milk and a number of other commodities. Expand, at the same time, the network of shops to sell cooked or half cooked foodstuffs.

The organs of industry, handicrafts and trade should increase the quantity of ready-made clothes, improving their quality and complying with the demands of workers of all ages, of all districts and especially for the countryside in general. Municipal services and those of the handicrafts should extend their service shops both in cities, in certain large agricultural cooperatives and in localities, so that some services ranging from tailoring to repairs of household utensils and pieces of furniture which are now being done at home. The Central Office of Communes should study and sum up the experience of the city of Tirana in expanding and utilizing public bath and laundry houses, so' that they be of better service to families.

In the countryside, where women are loaded with heavier work, not only household chores and bringing up children but also work in individual plots of ground, agricultural cooperatives should take steps to set up public ovens which could serve not only to bake bread but also to cook certain kinds of dishes for peasant families, public baths and laundry houses as the cooperatives in the Durres region have suggested, aqueducts to conduct water nearer to the dwelling quarters, collective cutting and transportation of firewood for each cooperative family, various workshops and so on.

The Party committees, state and economic organs in general, should make more efficient use of the major availabilities of every district, work center and agricultural cooperative. Experience gained heretofore has gone to show that with a little initiative and utilizing availabilities at their disposal a number of districts have created many facilities for household tasks.

Thus, by making a more equitable division of household chores among husband, wife and all the other members of the family and by gradually increasing measures to shorten the time necessary for household chores, there will be created more favorable conditions for women to render a larger contribution to social production and to the political and social life of the country and will enable them to develop from the political, cultural and professional point of view. This will mark a big step ahead towards the emancipation of women, giving a fresh impetus to their creative ability and raising the personality and role of women in our socialist society to a higher level.

MAKE THE PROBLEM OF WOMEN A PROBLEM OF SOCIETY AS A WHOLE

The Central Committee of the Party and Comrade Enver Hoxha have repeatedly stressed that the problem of women, affecting the fate of socialist construction, life and future of our country, is above all, a major problem of the Party.

Regional Party committees and grass-root organizations, carrying out the directives and recommendations of the Party Central Committee, have improved their work and have increased their concern about problems dealing with the emancipation of women. Better organized work and more concern about this matter is noticed particularly after the 5th Party Congress and Comrade Enver Hoxha's February 6th speech.

Nevertheless, the Political Bureau of the Central Committee asserts that major efforts should be exerted both by the Party committees as well as the grass-root organizations so that the problems of the complete emancipation of women may be better grasped in their breadth and depth.

In order to consolidate what we have achieved, in order not to return to where we started from, in order not take the struggle for the emancipation of women as a campaign, the Party should be on the alert, it should pile on more logs on the great revolutionary fire which has been kindled so that it may burn to ashes every alien concept which looks down upon and belittles women. Since the problem of the emancipation of women is a major one, it is essential that every separate aspect of it should be treated in all earnestness and become a problem of society as a whole.

On the forefront of the struggle for the emancipation of women, there should stand, as always, the members of the Party who should educate and lead the masses of the people by the example they and their families set. To be a communist, a fighter for the ideas of the Party on one hand, and to speak in general of the emancipation of women and do practically nothing to fight every day, everywhere and with all your efforts against customs and concepts which lie in the way of the complete emancipation of women, on the other — these are two irreconcilable things. It is to be regretted, but we have not few of such communists. There are those who, not understanding the line of the Party in this matter, remain slaves to conservative and backward influences. There are others, who align themselves with the slogans of the Party in words, repeat them even out loud, but in reality, they maintain a feudal and patriarchal attitude towards women in their homes and at work.

Comrade Enver Hoxha teaches us that one cannot be a communist while being a braggadocio, an insolent man and a petty bourgeois in the family considering the woman as a piece of property, as a household chattel. What kind of communist is he who resorts to a thousand ways to prevent the woman from participating in production and political and social life, who lacks confidence in her ability, or when it comes to trusting her with leading posts frowns and scowls, exerts pressure and puts a range of obstacles in the way? The views and attitude of these communists should be submitted for principled discussion of criticism in the Party organizations so that they may be helped and educated. They must understand that such an attitude of theirs is incompatible with their membership in the ranks of the Party, that their attitude is not a private, personal affair, but a problem of principle, for without the example of communists the problem of women cannot be properly solved with success.

Not only the communist but not even any other person be he a worker, a peasant or an intellectual, can call himself a man of the vanguard or a cultured man, if he does not maintain a correct attitude towards a woman, if he does not fight against everything which hinders her from occupying the place she deserves in society. Therefore, the Party is faced with the task of working on a frontal and massive way, but also with each person and family individually according to the particular conditions of every district, village or city quarter.

The question here is not to fight against men or women or to protect women from men. These ideas are alien to Marxism-Leninism, to our Party. The question here is to fight against backward views surviving from the past, particularly, among men, but also among women themselves. That is why the Party and society should be prepared to carry this fight through to the end in defense of women from all those who trample their rights underfoot.

In solving the problem of women an

important role should be played by the organizations of the masses, because on one hand, girls and women constitute a powerful force in their ranks and without the activization of boys and women, without their complete emancipation the organizations of the masses cannot accomplish the major tasks the Party has assigned to them properly, and, on the other hand, without the work of the organizations of the masses, without their active participation, the problem of women cannot become a major social problem in our country. Therefore, it is necessary to discard all thought and practice, according to which the problems of women are looked upon as problems of tb)e Organization of Women's Union alone.

The Democratic Front, the broadest political organization of the country, should be the platform from which to fight against old customs, religious dogmas and beliefs, which hamper the real liberation of women. Broad popular discussions of these problems at meetings of the Democratic Front should help clarify and persuade people that our socialist society cannot be duly developed without doing away with these concepts, just as it should create everywhere a stifling atmosphere for all those who trample underfoot the sacred law of our Party to protect the rights of the Albanian women.

Through its widespread branches in cities, towns and villages, the Democratic Front should outline a broad program of political and propaganda work, in order to put into practice new socialist norms, which deal with marriage contracts, facilities for women's household chores, women's active participation in the political and economic life, in the state and social cultural activities of the country, to stimulate and develop the initiative of the broad masses of people and to engage in concrete actions.

Bearing in mind that old customs pass from one generation to another, that they interfuse with the daily life and activity of people, becoming a habit and taking root in their world outlook the Party should devote special attention to the educative work with the young generation which should inherit all the virtues of our people and be protected and kept safe from every vice and backward custom which poison their minds and conscience. The heroic youth of our country, this colossal revolutionary and progressive force, should be in the front ranks of the struggle for the complete emancipation of women. How can our revolutionary youth tolerate their mothers, sisters, the comrades of their organizations to be trampled upon, to be discredited, to be treated according to mediaeval and religious laws? Our youth have always obeyed but one law. the law of the Party, the law of revolution and of the struggle, for the happiness of the people. That is why the Party trusts that all the youth of our country will be resolved, intelligent and courageous fighters for the great cause of fighting against everything that lies in the way of the complete emancipation of the Albanian woman. The Labor youth Union of Albania should devote special attention especially to the work with young women, to organize, educate and activize them in an all-round way. The young women who grow and are educated under condition of People's Rule, should not only be allowed to fall victims to bigotry and conservative ideas, but they should be turned into courageous fighters for the emancipation of the Albanian woman. To achieve this, it is imperative that an end be put to sectarism, which we meet with in the matter of their admittance to membership in the organization of youth, to put an end to the fanaticism which prevents them from taking active part in the life of the organization and to the formal work with young women. Of major importance in this respect is to draw as many young women as possible, especially from the mountain regions of the country to the mass actions of youth as to the Rogozhina-Fieri railway, to the highway in the Highlands, etc.

A major role regarding the problem of women evolves upon our schools, which as centers of ideological formation and scientific world outlook, as important educational means in the hands of the Party and of society, should lay the groundwork of sound proletarian precepts among young men and young women, should gradually enhance their personality. But at present our schools come short of filling these functions as they should. The Ministry of Education and Culture should delve deeper into the study of outlining correct scientific and pedagogical orientations in this field and of encouraging the adoption of revolutionary methods of teaching and of educating in general and of the moral uplift of youth in particular.

Women are a major component part of the working class of our country. Without activizing this force, without making it participate in all fields of life, the working class cannot play its role as the vanguard class which gives the tone to the whole life of the country. Therefore, the Trade Unions should devote special attention to the work of solving the problems of women workers, of their ideological, political, technical and professional uplift, of creating facilities and applying our legislative measures in economic enterprises. Trade Union organizations should be more active in drawing women to their activities and promote more of them to posts of responsibility helping them assert their personality not only as good workers and managers of production, but also as social activists. Trade Union organizations should be more particularly concerned about opening courses of qualification for women workers with a view to making them more efficient workers both in production and in political and social activity. The Trade Union should courageously raise their voice against any obstacle or bureaucratic procrastination in this matter.

The complete emancipation of women cannot be successfully brought about, if the women themselves and their organization, the Women's Union of Albania, do not raise their voice out loud and wage a persistent battle for it. We should admit that women themselves are the carriers of backward/ feudal customs and religious beliefs and superstitions. If the backward customs of selling off girls in marriage exist, if dowries and bridal trousseaux are widespread phenomena, this means that not only men but women, not only fathers but mothers also become often guardians of these mediaeval customs in our days.

The Women's Union of Albania in its capacity as the political organization of the masses of women under the leadership of the Party, has rendered great service to the country by enlightening the Albanian women politically, by mobilizing them extensively for all the activities of the life of our country. It has become a favorite organization of the women of our country and has always been an active auxiliary to our Party. But it should radically improve its work, in order to raise its political and organizational activity to the height which times demand so that it better tackle the great problems of the complete emancipation of women. Now that the cultural level of girls and women is being raised by all of them passing through 8-grade schooling, it becomes easier for the Women's Union organizations to intensify their activities also in the countryside.

The basic task of the women's organization remains also for the days to come to educate women to become resolved fighters to safeguard the rights they have won and to use these rights in the practical activities of their daily life. In every family we have more than one woman member of the Women's Union of Albania and each one of them should become a militant to carry the word of the Party, the progressive word, to establish new socialist customs and norms in the life of our family. The woman has a two-fold battle to wage: on the one hand, to cleanse her own conscience of everything that hampers her own progress, to fight against the backward ideas and gossip of the women themselves, on the other, to fight against the conduct and concepts of those who trample underfoot the rights of women and girls.

Work to educate and mobilize the widespread women activists should be one of the main concerns of the Women's Union of Albania, to make them stand on the forefront of struggle for the complete emancipation of women and, by their example, to draw to them and educate the broad masses of urban and rural women. The intellectual women activists of the city should carry on fruitful work in helping their rural comrades as agitators for, the line of the Party among the women masses.

Further enhancement of the role of the organization of the Women's Union of Albania in solving the problem's the Party is facing for the complete emancipation of women requires, above all, a deeper insight into its problems on the part of ' its leading organs and organizations, giving up for good the usual and injurious methods of practicism. The organizations of the Women's Union of Albania should make a better combination of the ideological educative struggle for the emancipation of women with the practical struggle of solving certain problems like that of a more cultured life in the countryside, of bringing up children, of cleaning the dwelling and working centers and so on. They should strengthen their relation with the broad masses of women, with their work and their daily life so as to have a closer view of the anxieties and opinions of the women and to organize their work to comply with the categories of women and their problems. The Women's Union of Albania should devote more attention to the women of the rural regions, to organize an all-round political and organizational, cultural and social assistance of them through sending time and again the best women, activists of the city to them.

The successful fulfilment of the grand tasks we are outlining at this plenum of the Central Committee depends to a large extent on the method of work of the Party organizations and committees as well as those of the masses, on their ability to organize the work of carrying them out. Therefore, further improvement of the revolutionary method and style of work, as the Party has repeatedly recommended, is one of the tasks of primary importance for us.

This requires that the Party organizations and committees as well as those of the masses should not view things superficially but should delve deep into their essence, they should not only engage in the practical struggle against customs that degrade women but to fight the concepts that have given birth to them and every cause which keeps them alive. The Party organizations and committees should keep away for good from empiricism which characterizes their work in many cases, and should delve deep both in the reality of our country and the materials of our Party and of the classics of Marxism-Leninism in order thus, to draw more theoretical generalizations from our practice and to open wider horizons both for themselves and for the people.

Considering that the further emancipation of women has both its ideological and its economic, organizational and administrative aspects, the combination of the ideological work with the economic and administrative measures, giving priority to the former, is of major importance to the method of the work of the Party organizations and committees, of the organizations of the masses and state organs. Political and ideological work outlined and supervised by the Party is the principal factor to fight with success all customs and concepts that lie in the way to the solution of the problem of emancipating women. But this should be as concrete and militant as possible. The Party has repeatedly spoken against customs that degrade women, but when the grass-root organizations of the Party indulged in criticism and self-criticism within the Party, when conflicting views came in to grips with one another in exchanges of opinions and discussions, when these problems were laid out openly and the people and the masses themselves rose up to fight, then the fire was lit and this unprecedented revolutionary drive burst forth. It behooves the Party to make wide use of this revolutionary method to form public opinion, to carry out the mass line in the class struggle for the emancipation of women.

With a view to making the problems of women the problems of the Party and society, with a view to organizing a more serious and scientific study of the problems of women, the Political Bureau has issued instructions to set up special commissions to work with women in the regional Party organizations and committees and under their direct supervision and proposes to the plenum to set up a similar commission at the Central Committee of the Party. The creation of these commissions should be understood aright and considered an organizational measure of major importance to help raise the role of leadership of the Party in the struggle for the emancipation of women and its concern about the problems of women. Their establishment should in no way push aside or replace the great role of the Women's Union of Albania just as it should not push aside and replace the role of the Party organization and Committees themselves.

The problem we are taking up at this plenum is of decisive importance to the further progress of our socialist Fatherland. The complete emancipation of women is one of the highest aims and one of the most fundamental tasks of our Party, in our struggle for the triumph of socialism and communism. Achievements attained so far in this field, opportunities that have been created by the socialist development of the country as a whole and the major revolutionary movement our Party has sparked of for the emancipation of women, allow us today to raise to a new and higher level our fight for the complete emancipation of women. The Central Committee of the Party expresses its deep conviction that our people, men and women, peasants and city folk, all, like sworn patriots, progressive and revolutionary people, united around the Party and under its leadership, will muster all their efforts and render all their contribution to ensure to women their full equality in life and to give them the place and great role pertaining to them in our new socialist society.

www.ingramcontent.com/pod-product-compliance
Lightning Source LLC
Chambersburg PA
CBHW070433290526
45791CB00005B/1952